GR
YARMOUTH
& GORLESTON
THEN AND NOW

Len Vincent

Photography by
David Bullock

John Nickalls Publications

This book is dedicated
to my granddaughters Anna, Kate and Beth

BY THE SAME AUTHOR
Great Yarmouth: A Portrait in Old Picture Postcards, Volume 1
Great Yarmouth: A Portrait in Old Picture Postcards, Volume 2

First published 2005
Copyright © Len Vincent/David Bullock 2005

ISBN 1 904136 26 5

Published by John Nickalls Publications
Oak Farm Bungalow, Sawyers Lane, Suton,
Wymondham, Norfolk, NR18 9SH

Designed by Ashley Gray and Printed by Geo. R. Reeve Ltd.,
9–11 Town Green, Wymondham, Norfolk NR18 0BD

CONTENTS

INTRODUCTION

IN THIS PICTORIAL TOUR of Great Yarmouth and Gorleston, the history of which has been well recorded elsewhere, it is hoped the scenes represented capture the aura of yesteryear as well as providing a snapshot of the town as it appears today.

As we might expect, there have been significant changes over the years, but not so many that the town of 'then' is unrecognizable from the town of 'now'. Because of its unique geography – a town built on a spit between river and sea – the large-scale expansion that has been a feature of other towns could not take place here. Yet changes there have been; many fine buildings and houses have become extinct through war damage or neglect, whilst others have been moved because they stood in the way of progress. Thus while we may look with a degree of fondness on yesterday's Yarmouth, it must be remembered that Great Yarmouth is an 'Ancient Town' and, as such, had large areas of poor housing which meant that slum clearance was both inevitable and welcome.

The photographs of Great Yarmouth and Gorleston as it appears today, stress the importance of well-thought and sympathetic planning to leave a heritage that others may enjoy in years to come.

Len Vincent
Great Yarmouth
2005

FRONT COVER: Haven Bridge, *c.* 1958 and 2005.

TITLE PAGE: Regent Road, *c.* 1952.

BACK COVER: Haven Bridge, *c.* 1955.

With regard to the photograph reproduced on the back cover, every effort has been made to trace the copyright holder but with no success. The author and publisher would be pleased to rectify any omission in a future edition.

TOWN HALL AND QUAY, GT. YARMOUTH.

THEN – TOWN HALL AND QUAY, *c.* 1900: A wide variety of transport is captured in this scene of the Quay and the Town Hall, which was built in 1882. Holidaymakers are evident, but the barrels and a railway track that extended to the fish wharf are a symbol of the fishing industry that the town once enjoyed. Two cabs are stationed outside the cabbies' hut.

NOW: Road transport that superseded rail is apparent as an articulated lorry nears the Town Hall. Large supply vessels moored along the quay show the port's connection to the oil industry. Traffic islands on the Hall Quay were introduced in the 1930s.

THEN – HALL QUAY, *c.* **1960:** Behind the boats moored along the quayside, the premises of Steward and Patteson can be seen. In 1793–4, John Patteson, a Norwich brewer, bought the North Quay brewery from W & J Fisher, with a Mr Steward joining the partnership in 1831. In its heyday there were over eighty outlets under the Steward and Patteson flag in the Yarmouth area. The business was eventually acquired by the Watney group, which closed the Yarmouth depot in 1969.

NOW: The three-storey building on the right of the picture, known as Quay House, was built in 1891 and was originally the home of the Lacon family who were brewers and bankers. For a hundred years it survived as a gentleman's club, commanding fine views of the river. For a short period it became a health and fitness centre and now trades as the Red Leaf Restaurant and Bar. The multi-storey office block, known as Havenbridge House, was built by local builders H A Holmes and Sons in 1973.

WENN LTD., NORTH QUAY, GREAT YARMOUTH.

3 TIMBER SHIPS DISCHARGING AT OUR WHARVES.

THEN – WENNS, *c.* 1930: Wenn Ltd, Timber Merchant and Box Manufacturer, had premises on South Quay, but due to constant flooding moved their business to North Quay, seen here with Norwegian ships unloading their cargo. Boxes were in great demand during the fishing season, whilst fruit and seed trays were also produced. In the late 1950s Jewson Timber Merchants acquired the premises.

NOW: Chimney pots are discernible, whilst to the right of the photo are the new buildings of Lovewell Blake Chartered Accountants. These buildings were opened in March 1998 by the High Steward of Great Yarmouth. The rounded canopies that once housed timber now provide cover for the fleet-hire vehicles.

Laughing Image Corner.

Atherton & Co. (Flood Series)

THEN – LAUGHING IMAGE CORNER, *c.* **1905:** Situated off North Quay, Laughing Image Corner derived its name from the two images that were ensconced on the front of one of the cottages situated there. This scene, taken during the 1905 floods, shows the White Swan Public House to the left. A railway crossing-gate can also be seen.

NOW: The White Swan public house remains practically unchanged in this view of North Quay. The new buildings featured from right to left are: the Postal Sorting Office built in 1977, the fully-automated Telephone Exchange and Great Yarmouth Magistrates' Court built in 1990. The access road between the Post Office building and Telephone Exchange bears the name 'Laughing Image Corner'.

THEN – CUBITT'S, FULLERS HILL, *c.* **1930:** Cubitt's Fish Merchants established their shop in 1879. It stood on the south side of Fullers Hill amidst a picturesque range of old shops and houses. Being the driest part of Great Yarmouth the first dwellings recorded there were in 1008. Fullers Hill derived its name from a landowner who had resided there.

NOW: 1971 saw the demolition of shops and houses on Fullers Hill to create a major highway into the town. One shop remains, now a Grade 2 listed building called 'Wheatleys', specialising in American collectables and seen here centre left of the picture. Early records show the shop as a haberdashery but in living memory it was a barbers and later a café.

DP. 4025 RACE COURSE, GT YARMOUTH

THEN – RACECOURSE, *c.* 1930: A course for horse racing on the South Denes was recorded in 1715 but it took over a hundred years before two meetings a year were established, and these on a small scale. In 1904, the Racecourse came under the control of the Borough Council and remained on the South Denes site until 1919. September 1920 saw the first race at its present site on Freemantle/Jellicoe Road. During the Second World War, the races were abandoned and the racecourse was taken over for military purposes.

NOW: In 2002, the Borough Council sold the lease of the Racecourse to 'Northern Racing', a private company. 14 May 2004 saw the unveiling of the £2.2million Lord Nelson Grandstand. The ceremony was performed by Britain's First Sea Lord, Admiral Sir Alan West, who, in true naval tradition, toasted the opening with a tot of rum. The Great Yarmouth Racecourse is now a multi-purpose complex catering for conferences, exhibitions, parties and wedding receptions.

THEN – THE IRON DUKE PUBLIC HOUSE, *c.* **1952:** The building of The Iron Duke Public House ceased during the war when the area came under military control. A builder's hut and temporary wooden fencing had yet to be removed when this photo was taken in early 1952. Once the Iron Duke was opened it meant that there was a total of eight establishments along Yarmouth's sea front under the Lacon sign. In the distance of an almost barren North Denes, the steam of a railway engine can be seen.

NOW: The first caravan park was sited on the South Denes in postwar years under the control of the Borough Council. In 1953, 12¾ acres of land on the North Denes, stretching from the railway line to the beach, was leased to a company called 'Yarmouth Seashore Caravans Ltd'. Upon the land were concrete emplacements built during the war for coastal artillery, these were converted into a shop, stores, offices and toilet blocks. Originally built to house 318 caravans, through successive proprietors the site has expanded and modernised to become one of the finest holiday complexes, commanding fine views of our shoreline.

THE POST OFFICE, NEWTOWN, GREAT YARMOUTH.

THEN – THE POST OFFICE, NEWTOWN, *c.* **1930:** A small girl poses outside the well-stocked windows of John Whiting's Post Office and General Stores, which stands on the corner of Churchill and Beaconsfield Roads. Ornate railings front the neatly uniformed row of terraced houses and a window cleaner's buckets and barrow add to this unfettered view of Beaconsfield Road.

NOW: The steady decline of general stores took place in the 'Fifties and only the cellar doors and postbox are reminiscent of its past. In 1963, R V and D T Futter Ltd, Yarmouth's oldest established firm of turf accountants acquired the premises, whilst houses have been adapted to individual taste and the car dominates the scene today.

THEN – BEACH STATION, *c.* **1910:** Branch railways were spreading across the country when the idea of a line from Great Yarmouth to Stalham was proposed in 1875. Thus, in May 1877, the first locomotive named *Ormesby* made its maiden journey from Beach Station to Caister. By 1881 the line had been extended from Stalham to North Walsham, merging in 1882 with the Eastern and Midland Railway, later part of the Midland and Great Northern network. Beach Station was a very popular station with holidaymakers from the Midlands in postwar years, however, it became uneconomical and was closed in February 1959.

NOW: An original platform roof column bearing the initials EMR, pictured to the right of the photograph, recalling its days as a railway station. 1961 saw its first use as a coach station, the site having been purchased by the borough. Housing seen in the distance known as the John Winter Court stands on the location of the former coal yards. The wall that once housed the yards can still be seen on the south-east corner of the housing estate.

THEN – 3 & 4 NORTH DRIVE, *c.* **1930:** In 1946, these premises were acquired and opened as St Louis' Convent Senior School until its closure in July 1971. Other Roman Catholic schools were situated in Albion Road and at 26 Nelson Road Central. The Senior School then became an independent day and boarding school with a high proportion of foreign students. Originally named North Drive High School, later to be known as The International High School, the buildings were demolished in 1990.

NOW: Once the site was cleared it was used as a car park during the summer months until the properties known as Esplanade Court were built in 1999. The penthouses and luxury apartments command a fine view of the beach and sea beyond. The flint and brick wall remain and electronic gates bearing the initials IHS are a recall of its past.

12.175. THE GARIBALDI HOTEL. GT YARMOUTH.

DOHLION SERIES

GARIBALDI HOTEL ANNEXE

THEN – GARIBALDI HOTEL, *c.* 1932: A small tavern once bore the name of Garibaldi and in 1888 it was rebuilt as a hotel. Its popularity grew and an annexe was added. Beyond the annex the chimney stack of Grouts, a silk and textile manufacturer, can be seen. Grouts established their mill on that site in 1815 and once employed 3,500 people. Lacons Brewery chimney is also visible.

NOW: Few areas of Great Yarmouth escaped damage during the 1939–1945 war and this corner of St Nicholas and Nelson Road was no exception. In 1954, flats replaced the Garibaldi annexe and in 1957 the top floors of the Garibaldi were removed. The Parish Church seen in the distance never had its grand spire replaced when restoration work began in 1957.

THEN – BRITANNIA PIER, *c.* **1906:** A French photographer's view of the Britannia Pier. An ornate drinking fountain stands to the left of the entrance. Many such fountains, in various forms, were a facility provided along the promenade. On the far right stands a garden bowl set on a terracotta-faced plinth which bears the Great Yarmouth coat of arms. This was one of many that graced the parade and from 1945 they began to disappear as a consequence of the growing commercialisation of the sea front.

NOW: The Britannia Pier, first built in 1858, has had a chequered history having been hit twice by ships and having sustained a number of fires over the years. A major fire in 1954 destroyed the pavilion and ballroom. The present theatre was built in 1957 and in the early days of television attracted many celebrities to spend a summer season entertaining there.

Valentines Series — St. Mary's R.C. Church, Yarmouth

THEN – ST MARY'S CHURCH, *c.* **1903:** Don Claudio Lopez was appointed to take charge of the Yarmouth Catholic flock in 1841, after coming to England from Spain in 1830. It was through his efforts that the church was built, which took two years to construct, and was completed in 1850 at a cost of £10,000. The church was designed by an architect by the name of Scoles and was built in the 14th century style.

NOW: In 1948, the Savoy Hotel and Restaurant was granted a beer-house licence and could cater for 500 on its first floor. It became a favourite haunt of the show business fraternity during the heyday of the postwar holiday seasons. Take note of the alterations to the church that were carried out in 1929.

THEN – MARINE PARADE, *c.* **1912:** The holiday season appears to have begun, hence the trader selling his wares from his barrow and the jockey scales on the right of this postcard. Some twenty years later the parade was widened and extended from the Britannia Pier to the Wellington Pier, seen here in the distance. The construction of the first terrace of houses on Marine Parade commenced in 1856.

NOW: The five million pound Marina Leisure Complex, on the left of the picture, was officially opened by the Olympic swimmer Duncan Goodhew on 15 June 1981. The Holkham Hotel, the white building on the right of the picture, having traded on its present site for over 120 years finally closed its doors in 1996 and awaits demolition.

THEN – CENTRAL BEACH, *c.* **1928:** Bathing machines along the shoreline, refreshment stalls on the beach, ice-cream sellers and open-top charabancs are captured in this view of the central beach. The buildings to the left of the bathing pool were public toilets and beyond these can be seen a concert party hall. This covered concert hall replaced Chapel's Singers Ring – a canvas-walled circle that could not keep out the elements.

NOW: Where once a man earned a living by pulling a barrow with notices attached, there now stands a circular advertising pillar. Pirates' Cove, a crazy-golf course, occupies the former bowling greens and illuminated fountains, which were built in 1937 and superseded the concert hall.

Copyright L. L.   Sunny Yarmouth.   ...th.90.

THEN – MARINE PARADE, 1926: This photograph, taken from the roof of the male cubicles of the outdoor swimming pool (built in 1922), shows the Royal Alfred and Royal Standard public houses, the Coastguard Station and the white open door of the lifeboat shed. The lifeboat shed was erected in 1859 at the then not inconsiderable cost of £400.

NOW: Amusement arcades dominate this stretch of Yarmouth's sea front. In 1965 the Tower building – comprising a hotel, nightclub, shops and an indoor ice-skating rink – opened on the site of the Coastguard Station. A major investment by local businessmen in 2002 has seen the complex change completely and is now known as 'Atlantis'.

The Jetty, Gt. Yarmouth.

THEN – THE JETTY, *c.* 1920: This view of The Jetty illustrates the popularity of 'promenading' in 1920. The picturesque kiosks in the foreground were erected in 1900 and behind the kiosk on the left can be seen one of the entertainments of the day – a rifle range. On the far right of this view of the Jetty can be seen one of the two cannons captured from Sebastopol, during the Crimean War. Before being located on the Jetty, the cannons had occupied a position on Hall Quay. In 1941, the cannons were removed from Yarmouth to be turned into scrap in order to aid the war effort.

NOW: Built of Portland stone, a twenty-foot memorial clock was erected in memory of all who died as a result of their captivity in Far East Prisoner of War camps during World War II. Lt. General A E Percival, a former GOC Far East, unveiled the monument in May 1953. The jetty shelters experienced severe damage during the 1953 floods and were demolished for safety purposes.

Marine Parade, Gt. Yarmouth.

46

THEN – MARINE PARADE, 1910: Three ladies, one carrying a parasol, stroll past the Royal Hotel in this 1910 scene of the Marine Parade. Charles Dickens is recorded as staying at the Royal Hotel in 1848. The gardens on the right were laid out in 1897. Looking at a traffic-free sea front it is hard to imagine that someone was fined for speeding at 8 miles per hour in 1899. In the distance a helter-skelter can be viewed on Britannia Pier.

NOW: The Royal Hotel is still a fine looking building, which has not yielded to some of the gaudiness of the Marine Parade. Further along, the dome of the Gem – now the Windmill Theatre – built in 1908, can be seen. (Absent in the postcard view). Tennis courts replaced the gardens in 1924 but these gave way to further commercial pressure in 1948 and various enterprises have taken place since.

THEN – PLEASURE BEACH, *c.* **1924:** Sand and duckboards surround the attractions of this late 'Twenties scene of the Pleasure Beach, when Mr Pat Collins was the lessee. The Figure of Eight Railway and Scenic Railway are featured. Covered stalls on the left housed coconut shies, darts and rifle shooting. The Hall of Mirrors, House of Fun and sideshows stood to the right.

NOW: In 1954, Botton Bros became the lessee of the Pleasure Beach and a new layout and resurfacing of the grounds began. The Scenic Railway brought from Paris in 1932 replaced the fire-damaged original. It was erected under the supervision of Mr Erich Heydrich and still takes pride of place amongst the ever-increasing thrill-seeking rides. In 1993, the relatives of Botton Bros bought the grounds and continue to improve the attractions.

LOWER FERRY, & FERRY HILL, GORLESTON.

THEN – LOWER FERRY, *c.* **1920:** There were two ferry crossing points on the River Yare known as Upper and Lower Ferries. Taking only a few minutes to cross, the Lower Ferry, shown here, was ideally situated to serve workers at Birds Eye, Hartmans, Erie Resistor and numerous smaller factories during the industrial development of the South Denes area which took place in postwar years. The advent of the family car saw the demise of the ferries.

NOW: Next to the white-painted Ferry Boat Inn, is situated Ferryside House. Formerly the home of Dr W Wyllys, it was purchased by the Corporation in 1947 and opened as a children's home in 1951. In 1960, it housed the offices of the Registrar of Births, Deaths and Marriages. 1976 saw the building of Gorleston's Fire Brigade quarters and its training and hose-drying tower stands to the right of Ferryside House.

THEN – METHODIST CHAPEL, *c.* 1928: The Primitive Methodist Chapel, which stood on Queen's Road, was built in 1867 with a seating capacity of over 600. During the Second World War it received a direct hit by enemy bombers. Demolition work began in 1954 and when the foundation stone of the chapel was opened it revealed a bottle containing coins and copies of the *Yarmouth Independent* and *Norfolk News* newspapers.

NOW: The two houses nearest the camera were built by H W Wright on the site of the former chapel. Scaffolding surrounds St James' church undergoing refurbishment to become the St James' Health and Resource Centre. Church services continue to be held in the church hall. Beyond the church stand the former premises of Mason's Laundry.

THEN – BLACKFRIARS ROAD, *c.* **1953:**
A combination of high tides and gale-force winds caused a major disaster on the east coast. Large areas of Great Yarmouth and Gorleston were completely flooded on the night of Saturday 31 January 1953. Breydon Water had burst its banks at several points and the river overflowed causing extreme damage to hundreds of homes throughout the borough. Our picture of Blackfriars Road shows a policeman and volunteers aiding a householder trapped on the first floor of his house.

NOW: The Blackfriars Tower still stands guard at the south end of the town. In the early 1970s, Great Yarmouth Borough Council sought a compulsory purchase order to improve the area. Flats now line the road where Gibbs butchers shop once stood. The clearance of Paradise Place and Adam and Eve Gardens revealed the town wall, seen here on the right.

THEN – TOWER TAVERN, BLACKFRIARS ROAD, *c.* 1926: Decorations adorn The Tower Tavern, which stood next to Gibbs the butchers shop, in earlier years, but what does the figure above the door represent?

NOW: This photograph, taken from the location of the Tower Tavern, looks north in Blackfriars Road. The old town wall and South East Tower are evident. In the distance is the much-acclaimed Tide and Time Museum which opened in 2004.

THEN – MIDDLEGATE STREET, *c.* **1900:** Formerly known as Gaol Street, Middlegate Street ran north to south from Hall Plain to Friars Lane. One of the main thoroughfares through old Yarmouth it was a busy bustling place with its wide range of houses, shops, beer-houses and factories. To the east and west of it were the rows, a densely populated part of Yarmouth. Heavily bombed during the last war, little of it remains today except a small area around the Tollhouse, which captures a flavour of the old street. Our picture shows the grocery store of H Dimmock, which stood next to the factory of Johnson and Sons, Oilskin Manufacturers.

NOW: In 1950, Middlegate was declared the number one reconstruction region in Great Yarmouth. An area, that was honeycombed with cellars, wells, fish steeps and small dwellings, is now a major housing estate. The keys to the first block of four houses built there were handed over in 1952.

THEN – CRANE HOUSE, *c.* 1907: The first crane was sited on South Quay in 1527. Crane House, seen in this view, was home to the YMCA from 1902 to 1934 before it became linked to the fishing industry serving as a welfare centre – primarily for Scottish fisherfolk – under the auspices of the Church of Scotland. At this time the building became known as St Andrew's House. In the 1960s, it reverted to its original name, when it housed various shipping agencies and a firm of architects.

NOW: Cars can be seen leaving the library access road. Previously on this site stood the Dutch Chapel (pictured in the postcard view). This structure was built in 1778 replacing an earlier building that was also known as The Dutch Chapel, with records dating back to the late 1500s. As a result of war damage the Dutch chapel was razed in 1946.

OFFICES OF THE GT. YARMOUTH GAS CO. IN KING ST.

THEN – GREAT YARMOUTH GAS COMPANY, *c.* 1920: Until its nationalisation in May 1949, the Great Yarmouth Gas Company had served the borough for 124 years. In the windows of its offices, built in 1912, various gas cooking ranges can be seen, advertised for as little as two shillings (ten pence) per quarter and fitted free of charge. The door on the left was for many years an entrance to a doctor's surgery.

NOW: In the mid 1960s, British Gas moved its offices to Regent Street and the vacated premises became a health food shop, later to become a frozen food centre. Today it houses a wine cellar and restaurant known as 'Kings Bar' and retains much of the original Gas Company frontage.

THEN – KING STREET 1923: Man and horse power are reminiscent of a much slower pace of life in this 1920s view of King Street. A street with a wide variety of shops selling everything from a single egg to complete house furnishings. A street where you could have a suit made and paid for on Friday and pawned on Monday. The tramlines seen here were removed in 1934 and one-way traffic introduced in 1954.

NOW: The bow-fronted house, a Grade II listed building was for over 200 years and until 1970 known as 'The Doctor's House'. Its close proximity to the hospital made it ideally situated for the many doctors and surgeons who practised there. The hitherto uninterrupted line of the west side of King Street was broken when in 1952 Nottingham Way and, in 1954, Yarmouth Way were created. Nottingham Way was named in recognition of the many visitors Yarmouth attracted in post-war years from that area.

THEN – GENERAL HOSPITAL, 1905: A hospital serving the community and its visitors had stood on Deneside since 1840. This postcard features the General Hospital, which was built in 1887. A horse drawn vehicle waits outside the main entrance and a nurse surveys the cameraman from one of the two balconies where, it was deemed, a patient could benefit from the fresh air by having their bed placed outside during the hours of daylight.

NOW: The hospital closed in 1982 and in the summer of 1984 work began to clear the site to allow these forty-two retirement premises to be built which is known as St George's Court. A wall nearby with the letters: 'NO PARKING – Doctor's cars only', can still be seen.

THEN – ST GEORGE'S PARK, *c.* **1900:** A peaceful scene as sheep graze in St George's Park which was created in 1866. The distinctive cupola of St George's Church, built in 1714 by John Price, towers above the fine houses fronting St George's Road.

NOW: St George's Park houses two memorials commemorating the dead of two world wars. The cenotaph featured here was unveiled by Prince Henry in 1922. Alexandra House, built in 1937, standing to the right of the monument was a Nurses' Home until the closure of the nearby hospital. It lay dormant for many years until its conversion into flats. St George's Church held its last service in 1959 and, fifteen years later, it was restored and opened as a theatre and arts centre.

THEN – CLOWES STORES, 1903: Delivery men and their assistants parade outside Clowes Stores, situated on Hall Quay at the foot of the bridge. The store traded there for many years until its closure in 1941 when the business transferred to Ipswich. From 1942 until 1960 the buildings became a temporary home for Great Yarmouth's library and part of the premises was used as an information bureau for Great Yarmouth Municipal Transport. *Picture courtesy of Peter Jones*

NOW: A complete change in style of architecture when the mid 1960s saw the rebuilding of 17 Hall Quay. Aldreds Estate Agents moved into their new premises in 1966.

THEN – GORLESTON HIGH STREET, *c.* **1935:** No parking problems in this early scene of Gorleston High Street. Next to Foxwell the drapery store stands the National Provincial Bank, then Hammonds the ironmongers and the Coliseum Cinema, which was built in 1913. The interior of the cinema had a refit in 1925, and the frontage was modernised in 1938. 1970 saw the closure and demolition of the cinema.

Picture courtesy of Peter Jones

NOW: Multi-national stores now occupy the site of the cinema and hardware stores, whilst the bank was modernised in 1969. However, Gorleston High Street maintains its charm by its many varied independent small traders.

THEN – THE TRAMWAY HOTEL, 1909: Livery stables and bowling greens are part of the facilities offered by the Tramway Hotel, first built in 1875. The landlord, a Mr Boyce, his wife, daughter and father-in-law were killed when the premises received a direct hit in June 1941. In December 1950 a prefabricated hut from a Suffolk airfield opened as temporary premises. *Picture courtesy of Peter Jones*

NOW: Standing next to the Tramway Hotel, built in 1957, is the Gorleston Library which opened in 1974 replacing the Carnegie Library and former Tramway sheds.

CLIFF HILL, GORLESTON.

THEN – CLIFF HILL, *c.* **1932:** An historic and picturesque part of Gorleston with a fine array of houses. Over the centuries, Cliff Hill has been known by many names including Prospect Hill, Pier Cliff Hill and Battery Hill. These names reflect the hill's commanding viewpoint with the latter taking its name from its use as the site where guns were placed during the Napoleonic Wars. Perhaps the most evocative name that Cliff Hill has been known by is Deadman's Hill – a reference to the suspected murder of a rich man who was being ferried ashore by boatmen who were residents of the hill. The story has it that the boatmen brought back the rich man's valuables – but not the rich man.

NOW: A bow-fronted house built in the mid 'Fifties replaces two cottages damaged by enemy action during World War II and other more subtle changes to properties have taken place over the years.

THEN – CLIFF HOTEL, *c.* 1929: A massive fire, described as a towering inferno, completely destroyed the Cliff Hotel on Boxing Day 1915. Our 1920s view shows the hotel built to replace it. The ladies cloche hats and gentlemen's white trousers and shoes encapture this 'Twenties scene.

NOW: A balcony and canopy have been lost during further improvements to the hotel, which continues to trade as the Cliff Hotel, as it has done since 1897.

THEN – WILLIAM IV, *c.* 1912: Residents and boatmen pause for the photographer who captured this scene in the early 1900s. In the background stands the William IV Public House, which suffered a major fire in 1881. A lookout tower is an interesting feature of the public house, the lights of which were a guide to ships prior to the red and green lights being installed on the North Pier. *Picture courtesy of Peter Jones*

NOW: The present public house, now known as the King William, stands twenty yards in front of the old William IV and was built in 1904 by Bullards the Brewers. Houses in the distance can be recognized in both pictures.

THE HARBOUR, GORLESTON.

THEN – THE HARBOUR, GORLESTON, *c.* **1926:** Two cabs and a brake are in the foreground of this early 'Twenties postcard scene, whilst in the distance a pleasure steamer leaves the quayside to head its way to Great Yarmouth Town Hall, a service which started in 1894 and was discontinued in the 'Fifties. Other signs of travel are the tramlines. Sailing boats complete this picture of Brush Quay. Note the lookout tower.

NOW: The lighthouse, built in 1886, still stands overlooking this changed scene of Brush Quay and the more leisurely means of travel have disappeared. An increase in development of the South Denes is evident.

THEN – SPRINGFIELD ROAD, *c.* 1907: The message on the reverse of this card sent in June 1907 reads: "Dear Daddy, isn't this a good view of our road? We are enjoying ourselves very much. Kate is waiting to bath me as mother is going to church. We must be done early. Lots of love from us all, your loving daughter, Grace." This photo has a quiet Sunday air about it.

NOW: Terrace houses began to lose their uniformity and balanced appearance in the 'Fifties when DIY and home improvements took hold. Out went the sash windows, to be replaced by top-hung or side-vent openers and picture windows. Solid doors gave way to half or fully glazed doors. Pebble dashed, coloured exterior walls and later stone cladding began to appear, thus altering the facade of streets that had seen little change in decades.

THEN – GORLESTON STATION, *c.* 1930: Serving as a link from Yarmouth Southtown to Lowestoft, Gorleston railway opened in 1903 on land that was once known as Stone Piece. Later that year a connection to Yarmouth Beach Station was made via the Breydon Swing Bridge, until 1953 when the Swing Bridge was closed. The coastal line closed in May 1970. The Gorleston Station buildings were used as a Driving Licence Test Centre for a short period but eventually the buildings became derelict.   *Picture courtesy of Peter Jones*

NOW: Following the line of the former rail track, construction of a road from Southtown to Gorleston was begun in April 1991. Over 230,000 cubic metres of earth were moved to create the Inner Relief Road, taking traffic away from Gorleston's High Street. Built at a cost of over 15 million pounds the two-and-a-half-mile road that links the A12 to the A47, opened in September 1993.

THEN – EAST ANGLIAN SCHOOL, 1936: The East Anglian School for Blind and Deaf Children stood on 17 acres of land and was opened by the Earl of Leicester in 1912. The school closed in 1940 and its pupils were evacuated to Glamorgan, returning in 1946. The swimming pool featured here was opened in 1936. The school closed finally in 1985.

NOW: The East Anglian School was demolished in 1990, and a housing estate and St Mary's Roman Catholic Primary School now occupy the site. On the gates of the new school is a commemorative plaque to the East Anglian School, which was unveiled in 2003.

CHURCH RD. GORLESTON. (N)

THEN – CHURCH ROAD, *c.* 1933: A motor vehicle passes the 1884-built Church Road Infants and Junior School and advertising placards adorn the walls of Mrs Glissold's grocers shop. A lamp standard and telegraph poles standing on the kerbside all add to this nostalgic view of Church Road. The school has had a chequered history, in its early days it was listed as a council school (cookery and laundry centre) whilst ending its days as an annexe to the College of Further Education.

NOW: Houses built in 1996 now occupy the former site of the school, whilst in the distance cottages that stood between Bulls Lane and Priory Street have been replaced by the flats of Da Volls Court, built in 1965.

THEN – GORLESTON HIGH STREET (LOOKING NORTH), *c.* **1928:** Houses nestle between the Coliseum building and the National Provincial Bank's premises in this almost rural scene of Gorleston High Street. A tram trundles past the tramway depot. Pickfords removal and stores advert has pride of place on the hoardings above the shops at the end of the High Street known for many years as Nortons Corner, a reference to a well-established local firm of tobacconists whose shop stood there.

NOW: The straight and unaesthetic lines of modern architecture are apparent, whilst the plethora of chimneys on Lowestoft Road remain the same in this photograph of Gorleston High Street looking north.

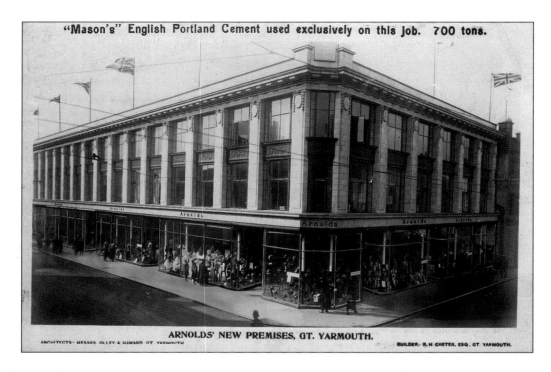

"Mason's" English Portland Cement used exclusively on this job. 700 tons.

ARNOLDS' NEW PREMISES, GT. YARMOUTH.

ARCHITECTS:- MESSRS. OLLEY & HAWARD, GT. YARMOUTH.   BUILDER:- R. H. CARTER, ESQ. GT. YARMOUTH.

THEN – ARNOLDS' DEPARTMENT STORE, 1922: In 1869, the Arnold brothers Frank and William started trading at 180 King Street where the business flourished and soon they bought the corner shops on Regent Street and King Street. A large fire gutted the premises in 1919. This postcard shows their new building. The business merged with Debenhams in 1935 but continued to trade under the Arnolds name. The restaurant, which was situated on the second floor, advertised 'An up-to-date Orchestra' and 'Well-appointed Men's Smoking Rooms'.

Picture courtesy of Peter Jones

NOW: In 1972, Arnolds changed their name to Debenhams which it traded under until its closure in 1985. Later the goods entrance and part of the store were demolished; the rest of the store was subdivided into smaller shops. It is interesting to note the change of style in the window dressing.

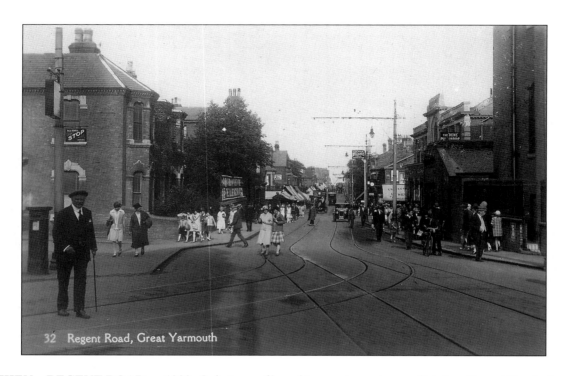

32 Regent Road, Great Yarmouth

THEN – REGENT ROAD, *c.* 1933: Only two cafés and two restaurants were listed on Regent Road when this photo was taken in the early 1930s. A much wider range of goods were available then including baby carriages, hats, flowers, motorcycles, musical instruments, pianos and sheet music. Doctors and Dentists were among the residents of the fine houses that interspersed the shops. Two billiard halls are advertised; 'The Dene' and the 'Luciana', which was situated in Jubilee Place, an alley that connected Regent Road to South Market Road.

Picture courtesy of Peter Jones

NOW: The lower floor level of the once dignified terraced houses that fronted Regent Road has given way to gift shops, restaurants, take away food outlets and clothes shops, making the road a bright, but gaudy, avenue to attract visitors. Only a few businesses of earlier years have survived. A CCTV camera surveys the milling crowds.

THEN – REGENT CINEMA, _c._ 1930: The Regent Variety and Picture Theatre opened on Boxing Day 1914 with a seating capacity of 1,679. It was built by a consortium of local businessmen, headed by F H Cooper, a cinema magnate, and showed its first talking film on 19 August 1929. On either side of the entrance were oak-panelled tea-rooms.

NOW – REGENT THEATRE: Not only a change to the façade but also in entertainment when, in 1948, the Regent Theatre became a bingo club. During the 1930s there were seven theatres in Great Yarmouth. In 1989, part of Regent Road was pedestrianised. Donald Nobbs, the local photographer's shop, can be seen in both pictures.

THEN – DENESIDE, *c.* 1934: Two fascinating milk floats stand outside the wholesale department of the Norfolk Dairy Association premises situated on Deneside. Their retail shop, known as The Model Dairy, was situated at 30 King Street. The business ceased trading there in 1937. *Picture courtesy of Peter Jones*

NOW: Part of the old town wall remains behind the former dairy. The conical roof of The Pinnacle Tower, which is situated at the rear of Park House on Alexandra Road, can be seen from the goods entrance of British Home Stores, featured here.

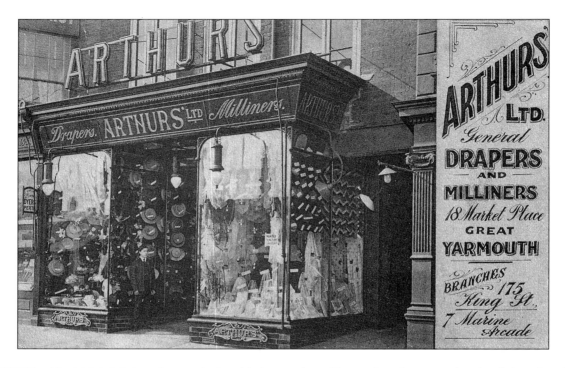

THEN – 18 MARKET PLACE, *c.* 1924: With the number of lamps focusing on Arthurs' Ltd shop front it would be hard to miss their display of hats and millinery in this 1920s view. Arthurs finished trading in the early 'Thirties, but the premises remained home to various drapers and furnishers for many years, trading under such names as Austins, Kerridges and Brown & Co. The passage of Row 32 and the ornate plinth of The Market Tavern are also shown.

Picture courtesy of Peter Jones

NOW: The Market Tavern, previously known as the Growler Public House, but originally called The Kings Head, lends itself to a continental ambience with its outside tables and chairs. The former hotel maintains its original frontage in the ever-changing face of the Market Place. Row 32 bears a plaque as Kings Head Row. Arthurs premises are now occupied by Specsavers.

THEN – LACONS BREWERY, *c*. 1950: Brewing began on this site in 1640. In 1760, it became known as Mr Laycon's Brewery and from that time, until its merger with Whitbread, the Lacon family controlled it. The imposing buildings dominated Brewery Plain and although damaged in an air raid in 1942 were rebuilt in 1948.

NOW: The Palace Bingo buildings were the purpose-built premises of Tesco, having previously traded in a smaller store in the Market Place. Expanding still, they moved to an out of town trading centre in September 2002. Forty-two flats built in 1980 at a cost of £458,000, bearing the name of Falcon Court, occupy the remainder of the site. The falcon, being the trade symbol of Lacons, can be seen above the arch in the brewery picture. Also pictured is the Wrestlers Arms where Lord Nelson and Lady Hamilton stayed after the Battle of Aboukir Bay in 1860.

NORTHGATES STREET, GT. YARMOUTH.

B.P.C.
COPYRIGHT.   GT YARMOUTH.

THEN – NORTHGATE STREET, *c.* **1930:** There is plenty of activity in this early 1930s scene of Northgate Street. Just beyond the road sweeper stands a cart complete with milk churn. Safety regulations are not a concern for the lamp cleaner and cycles are a common mode of transport.

Picture courtesy of Peter Jones

100

NOW: White lines replace the tramlines, which were removed in 1934, and the car dominates the scene. The shellfish mongers shop front (nearest to the camera in the 1930s shot) has been transformed to encompass the house.

THEN – METHODIST TEMPLE, *c.* **1905:** Yarmouth's first Wesleyan Chapel stood in Row 8 near Fuller's Hill and was opened by John Wesley in October 1873. Pictured is the Methodist Temple and its schoolroom situated at Priory Plain whose foundation stone was laid in 1875. The temple had a seating capacity for 1,200. Its closure came about in 1963.

NOW – METHODIST TEMPLE: The temple was demolished in 1972 and ten years later the town centre relief road called Temple Way opened, creating a link from Fuller's Hill to Alexandra Road. The house to the left of the photograph stands on the site of the former schoolroom.

THEN – MARKET PLACE, 1911: Crowds line the Market Place and beyond to watch a parade celebrating the coronation of King George V in June 1911. On the left stands the Fishstall Public House which finished trading in 1971, the Old Blue Coat Charity school built in 1713 and compulsorily closed in 1891, seen here trading as a bazaar. The buildings facing the camera housed a bank, a doctor's residence and Hedges, a national shoe retailer.

NOW: Trading began at the new Market Gates shopping precinct in 1975. The Market Place became pedestrianised in 1988 and our picture taken in 2005 shows the recent £90,000 refurbished entertainment area with its large information screen standing beneath the clock of the Lloyds TSB building. In the distance the church tower of St Spyridon, formerly St Peter's church, built in 1833 can be seen.

ACKNOWLEDGEMENTS

My thanks to Michael Bean and his colleagues at Great Yarmouth Library, Simon, Alison Melton and Tim Vincent, and finally to Peter Jones for the loan of his postcards on pages 64, 66, 68, 74, 80, 88, 90, 94, 96 and 100 – and for his friendship over the years in our shared hobby.

Len Vincent

ABOUT THE AUTHOR AND PHOTOGRAPHER

THE AUTHOR: Len Vincent was born in Great Yarmouth and has lived there all his life. He spent his early working life in the glass trade before National Service took him to Trieste for two years. Upon his return he continued working in the glass industry before moving on to the Royal Mail.

His interest in old postcards began in 1970 whilst walking along Gorleston High Street and spotting a postcard of Yarmouth's yesteryear in a shop window.

Len has been a member of the Norfolk Postcard Club for many years and is a past Chair.

He is the author of *Great Yarmouth; A Portrait in Old Picture Postcards, Volumes 1 and 2.*

THE PHOTOGRAPHER: David Bullock was born in Gorleston and still resides there. At the age of seventeen he joined the Merchant Navy and after seven years at sea found employment with British Gas, remaining with them for thirty-five years. He now works part-time at the James Paget Hospital.

Woodcarving and photography have been amongst his hobbies for many years and he specialises in portrait photography.

LOCAL TITLES PUBLISHED BY JOHN NICKALLS PUBLICATIONS

A Garland of Waveney Valley Tales A compilation of illustrated tales from Suffolk of yesteryear.

A Level Country Sketches of its Fenland folk and history.

A Pharmacist's Tale The joys, delights and disappointments encountered preserving pharmacy history.

Curiosities of Norfolk A county guide to the unusual.

Curiosities of Suffolk A county guide to the unusual.

Great Ouse Country Sketches of its riverside folk and history from source to mouth.

Ladies of Distinction in Northamptonshire A pot-pourri of charismatic women from all walks of life.

Melton Constable, Briston & District – Book One A portrait in old picture postcards.

Melton Constable, Briston & District – Book Two A further portrait in old picture postcards.

Nature Trails in Northamptonshire A series of illustrated walks.

Newmarket, Town and Turf A pictorial tour.

North Norfolk A portrait in old picture postcards.

Norwich – Then and Now A look at the city through old postcards and modern photographs.

In and Around Norwich – Then and Now A further look at Norwich and district.

Harwich, Dovercourt and Parkeston – Vol 3 A further selection of old picture postcards.

Norwich – Then and Now A third selection of old picture postcards.

Robber Barons and Fighting Bishops The Norman influence in East Anglia.

Shires, Sales and Pigs The story of an Ely family of Auctioneers. George Comins, 1856–1997.

Suffolk's Lifeboats A portrait in postcards and photographs.

S'Wonderful A symphony of musical memories.

'Smarvellous More musical memories.

Tipple & Teashop Rambles in Northamptonshire A series of illustrated walks.

Walks in the Wilds of Cambridgeshire A series of illustrated walks.

Wicken: A Fen Village A third selection of old pictures.

For a comprehensive list of all publications please visit:
www.john-nickallspublications.co.uk